MUSINGS OF THE QALB

A WANDERER'S REVERIE

RAZIN

Made with ♥ on the Notion Press Platform
www.notionpress.com

"To the ones who were chosen to shed light upon the chambers of my heart, your radiance has painted my world with the hues of gratitude and warmth."

Contents

Contents

Contents

Author's Note

بسم الله الرحمن الرحيم

I have connected the dots and drawn a line, creating a book of musings—the reflections of a heart, deemed a wayfarer, lost upon the vast expanse that belongs to this humble being. These fictional diary scribbles are like whispers to the wind, the moon, the skies, and ultimately to the One who owns it all.

As you traverse the pages of this book, you will encounter both spiritual and religious content. However, bear in mind that these are my descriptions from the nectars of the flowers of this beautiful faith that I have tasted, and I acknowledge my vulnerability to error. Feel free to correct me, but refrain from accepting anything regarding this faith from me, without verification and contemplation.

Moreover, don't attribute the characteristics you find in these words to the pen that wrote them. The goodness you perceive is merely a reflection of the goodness you wish to see in yourself. Any advice shared is first directed at me and then to you. Let not the sin of misperception add to my list of sins.

May you discover a haven of warmth and sunshine within the pages of this book. May your breaths tingle your heart, lighten your burden, and elevate your spirits. I humbly request a room in your precious duas.

-Razin

Vocabulary

- *Qalb (قَلْب): Heart. In a spiritual context, it refers to the innermost core of a person, encompassing thoughts, feelings, and intentions.*
- *Sabr (صَبْر): Patience or endurance. It refers to the ability to persevere and remain steadfast in the face of challenges or difficulties.*
- *Qadr (قَدَر): Divine destiny or decree. It encompasses the belief that everything that happens in the universe is preordained by Allah.*
- *Tawakkul (تَوَكُّل): Trust and reliance on Allah. It is the act of putting complete trust in Allah while also taking necessary actions.*
- *Imaan (إِيمَان): Faith or belief. It is the fundamental concept in Islam, representing the acceptance of the core tenets of the Islamic faith.*
- *Shukr (شُكْر): Gratitude or thankfulness. It involves acknowledging and appreciating the blessings bestowed by Allah.*
- *Ikhlaas (إخْلاص): Sincerity or.purity of intention. It involves doing actions solely for the sake of Allah without seeking praise or recognition from others.*
- *Qalam (قَلَم): Pen. It is often used metaphorically to represent knowledge, wisdom, and the act of writing or recording information.*

The Wanderer's Reverie

And by the window side of the caravan, I saw this young man, deeply lost in the vastness of the desert that covers all the horizon. His body looked weak, but his face glowed with a sense of serenity. He was holding a beautifully ornamented pen, and a brown vintage diary in his hands. I had this yearning to feel the weight of his heart, that I asked him, "what makes you different from the rest of the people I've ever met my dear young man?".

"Perhaps, you never met a poet." said he.

"Ah, I have not. What makes you write while the rest of the people here, even when the camels are tired of this long journey? What is the story behind that young wild soul of yours?", I asked.

"Oh me. I, was silenced by the eyes of the world. I was silenced for a long time that all the words grew and saturated inside of me and choked me. And then suddenly one day they broke out of me as poetry. All my veins and its blood got infused with words and the symphonies of the universe such that, I bled poetry and all my scars from those wounds turned me into a poet.

And now when I see the eye seizing beauty of the creations of god, my tongue can't express but my heart leaks as poetry. So I write, despite how tired I am. Neither the place nor the people ever held me back from writing. I don't wish to be read but I wish to leave what flows out of me, for these papers sometimes doesn't have ink in it but blood stains from how I had to carve my heart out to write in some poetry."

And that was how I met the poet, on my journey through the deserts of my heart, on my barren lands, I saw him by the corners magically sowing poetry on the corners of my heart, giving solace to my burning soul, giving a voice to my silenced existence, giving power to my weakest parts.

And his musings echoed in my Qalb, spawning flowers within, taking me further apart from this dunya that is delusional, to a world where lies all the hopes and glitters for today and the rest of the days to come. And I took hold his vintage diary, and read from it, the "Musings of the Qalb".

1. Journey of Divine Love

I know that I am but an uninvited guest,
in your grasslands, but I am here to drop flowers
over the wild shrubs and trees in here,
to adorn every part of your lives with
something you kept forgetting about.

I am here to bring the scent of faraway lands
that lie beyond all these oceans and skies,
from where I learn and bring words to you,
so that you can feel all that I feel,
the feel of a divine love that stirs up your heart
and makes your being whirl into a bottle
filled with the nectars of
blissful patience brewed with tawakkul.

I trespassed into your gardens to write
on the petals of your flowers,
so that when you shall fall lost in a strange love
and when the butterflies trapped inside your lungs
fly you to the gardens, you'll be able to read out loud
that the love of Allah is the greatest of love.

I am no scholar nor fit to be called pious,
I am merely a sinner, beading words into wonderlands
where I wish to contribute for you to get lost enough
to fall into the truest of paths.

I am not a guide but wish to be a signboard,
a fallen tree upon the wrong road,
a wind that directs
the sail away from the storms.

With every word, I try to weave a tapestry of dreams,
rivers of roses and starry, moonlit streams,
so that you will float upon it and find yourself stumbling
upon the gateway to the most beautiful of lands,
the land of taqwa, where you could fill the voids in you
with the love for Allah and a love for whatever He loves.

I wish that you wither away from the worries
and weights of this world and
join me in my world of imaginations
so that we could pursue our true purposes.

I don't wish for you to
keep me alive in your memories,
but I wish that you walk upon
these paths that I melted words
and painted yellow and rented fireflies,
so that you could walk and
end up opening the sealed doors
of your heart that is filled with divine love.

2. Along the expanse of my heart

And today, I was a storyteller of all seasons,
riding upon my beloved horse, chasing sunsets,
passing through villages
and gathering the children to tell them stories.

I told them of how the moon
chases people with beautiful hearts,
waiting for them to whisper to me in excitement
of how they think they secretly got a beautiful heart.

I am a reader of eyes and wrinkles, of the stories
that the faces tell as they get lost in dancing
with the cold breeze at the window sides of the caravans.
I travel to reminisce about fragrances
upon which I have stored memories.
I travel in search of colors
for the half-painted canvas that lies within me.
I travel to run into rains and smell coffee in the streets.

I travel along the expanse of my heart,
and I whisper in my prayers, asking Him to broaden it,
cleanse it, and beautify it,
so that I could forever be a traveler
in this heart of mine—
traveling in search of the beauty of its Rabb,
living off the sweetness that comes with His remembrance.

3. A madman's treasure

I yearn to sit beside the skies and weave
a thousand words, to souls and hearts, I'd leave.
To converse with unheard inner voices, untold,
befriending stories and prayers, a thousandfold.

I yearn to build monuments, a thousand or more,
for beautiful thoughts that my mind did store.
But at times, I realize, lost in oblivion's schemes,
I'm merely a madman, with a bag of dreams.

Words that escaped from garden's walls, it seems,
fell from the stars, into rivers, like vivid dreams.
Illuminating oceans, they now reside within,
a madman's treasures, a bag of words, my kin.

4. Stranger

"Who do you think you are?" they asked.

"I am but a prisoner of this temporal world
and all its possessions.
My soul is merely a traveler,
destined beyond the horizon,
Where suffering ends, and hearts
shall peace in their return to home.
I am naught but a collection,
of oscillating atoms and emotions,
I am one among the infinite
fragments of the universe,
Without which the world and
its story would remain incomplete.
I am unimportant to those who know me,
yet vital to the universe.

I am a stranger to every land,
but a relative to all the skies.
A guest in the hearts,
but a resident of the moon."

5. Metaphors for you

I would sew metaphors for you,
the ones carrying beautiful hearts,
as people walking amidst vast gardens,
Gazing at the whimsical skies,
embracing hearts like snowfall,
all within their inner walls.

But beyond the skies of your heart
lies an entire universe,
With glimmering stars and whirling planets,
Galaxies of immaculate beauty,
Swirling moons and colorful rings,
All inside you, just like your heart.

A universe found when you
look beyond eyes clouded by the dunya,
when you close your eyes and feel
The clutch of the heart, and call upon Him,
The one divine, who is Al-Fattah.
In the breath that burdens the ground in prostration,
And the eyes that brim with drops of love and hope,
In His plans, lies the sweetest fragrance.

A sweetness that comes with pain,
Embracing happiness, tasting like the water
When a lost bedouin finds an oasis
In the colossal desert.

Then, your whole being will feel
Like withholding a universe,
With stars, moons, and trapped light
Dancing within you, brimming with love
for the eternal world.

Aligning your soul to seek truthful guidance,
A love too heavy to carry,
Pulling you deep within yourself,
To the bottom of your heart.
There, you discover your true fitrah,
Covered by the dirt of this dunya.
In that place, the thirst of your soul shall be quenched,
Finding solace unfound
in any corner of your constrained world.

6. The castle of my heart

I had already left the castle of my heart,
for there was no room in there without suffocation.
All the secret chambers in there were hoarded with dirt,
and the treasury was not filled with gold
but with the words that some passersby left.

The halls were filled with the fragrance of some pure hearts
whose absence always brought pain.
The throne had became a graveyard
where a hundred myself has been buried.
So I deserted the castle and sealed the gate
with the fallen skies of my heart,
so that one day I could come back,
break into those walls
and turn the ruins of my memoir
into a museum of woven words
that I weaved with the strings of wild musings.

7. Walking toward the skies

Indeed, I have fallen in love,
with my thirst to express
how stars whirl atop my heart
when I'm left alone within myself.
I've fallen in love with
words and the endless universe,
that is being created within my mind.

Fragments of my soul fall apart
in all the places I go,
and it is with a pen that I
pick up the pieces of me
and clean the dirt that sticks to it.

Now, far from my homeland,
I carry my universe on my back
and walk to unknown lands,
to speak to the entire world
about what I feel when
light falls upon my heart
through the broken window.

Even in this captivity,
my mind has walked away from me
through the cracks in these walls,
in pursuit of building
much more beautiful skies,
so that when I break free
from the shackles of this dunya,
I can happily cloud walk upon them.

8. Wordsmith of the heart

I had exiled the poet from the village of my heart,
for each time I picked up the weapons to challenge the world,
his ballads melted my sword and armor, leaving me weak.

I had banished the poet,
but he lingered by the gates of my village,
singing a song of love and melancholy that echoed loud.
The wars within could never subjugate me,
but his words imprisoned me without shackles.

He conquered the skies that reside within me,
weaving a moon with his words and placing it there.
I once thought the poet was weak,
but then I realized he was the one who weakened me.

So, I opened the gates for him,
and now he is my swordsmith,
forging swords with words
that wound without leaving scars.
I opened the gates for him,
and now he is my artisan,
rafting doors with words on the ground
that open to the seven skies.

9. Galloping through dreams

In the realm of my day dreams, I harbor a desire:
to vanish from the minds of all who dwell in here,
to become a stranger to these enchanted lands.
To stroll the streets, and a wistful nostalgia
would stir within the passersby, an elusive memory
of a face long forgotten yet oddly familiar.

To craft letters infused with glittery words,
gifting them to radiant souls, seeking
a fleeting glimpse of their gleeful eyes.
Adorning all the way with hanging moons,
drawing galaxies upon the walls
and whispering to people to look at the stars.

With a satchel in hand,
blabbering stories to my big fat cat,
traversing through borders,
imagining ethereal realms
in between coffee shops and book stalls.

Galloping through dreams,
hearts, cites and serene countrysides.

To be unknown, yet at the same time to carry
the mysterious scent of a known one to all the world.

10. The wind took away my secrets

The wind took away my secrets,
the soil buried my worries
and the water cleansed my dirt.
And suddenly everything went still,
the trees stopped its whispers,
the wind halted its dance,
the clouds disappeared and only the crescent moon
was seen in the dark sky.

The rhythms of the heart resonated
with the waves that the moon radiated.
And the moon that lies as a spot of light
in the midst of this infinite darkness
reminded me of a heart that is able to illuminate
itself from within by the light of faith.

Perhaps, if there are breathes
left for me to take tomorrow,
there'll surely be a purpose
woven to every single one of them.

Each one would be a piece of land that floats
in the sky that gives me opportunity
to take a step closer to my Rabb.
Each one of them would be
the pages of my destiny that would be unfolded
as the stars and the moons float around the galaxies.

And hundreds of lands might be awaiting for me,
to bring roses to my soul.
There might be a thousand people
whose books would be having my name
engraved in between its page,
who'll be carrying hearts
that'll adorn the streets of my life.

Who knows what tomorrow holds,
except the One who gave a moon to all the skies,
the One who wrote every story in the most mysterious
yet in the most beautiful of ways.

With His will, you and I
who feed upon some leaves in this moorland
shall turn into the butterflies of tomorrow
that'll fly around the whole dunya.

With His will, we shall turn into the rainbow
that appears in the skies of someone who expects rain.
With His will the worries of today shall fade away,
and the scent of roses shall blend into our souls.
With His will, we shall reunite, in paradise.

11. These streets have grown old, so did I

These streets have grown old, so did I.
The things that I once loved,
have all now vanished away.
There was a bangle maker in that corner of the street,
we used to make bangles and talk till the sun sets.
There was a chaiwala nearby the sweets shop,
whose chai felt like taking a sip from the heavens.
The street lights had embroideries
as same as my sister's blue churidar.

I was a friend of this street,
perhaps more than a friend,
A son, a brother.
I used to paint the flawed walls in here,
I used to draw in the footpaths with chalks,
I used to sing to the cats.
Walking down this street used to

fill my lungs with happiness
and with the smell of biryani.
Each person here was so rich in their heart,
that they had their own moon to their eyes.

But now, now this street is deserted,
abandoned, turned into ruins.
When I walk in here,
I step on the bricks of my broken home.
I grew up and tried living in other's shoes in here,
And in the process I lost my own shoes.

Now, I doze off on the corners of this street,
daydreaming of how beautiful this street would have been
if those dark clouds hadn't fallen from the sky into here.
The cloud that spat dirt over my innocence.

I wish that the people here had never left,
so that we could have decorated this broken street
just like how we used to decorate every other broken thing.

My limbs have now lost their strength,
my soul has now grown weak,

and this street that lies
in between my heart and my mind,
is now waiting to be perished.
But then the fireflies do visit here,
to sit upon the broken pieces,
waiting for me to chase them.

But now, these streets have grown old, and so did I.

12. Beauty in suffering

I adore it every time I see little ones,
sitting by the window panes, their eyes wandering,
across streets, faces, and the vast skies above,
for within their eyes, an untainted world gleams.

I melt when a burdened soul graces me with a smile,
for in their smiles, I gauge their unwavering faith,
they never yield to the trials they face,
but instead, praise the Author of their fate.

The beauty of Allah's creation knows no bounds,
it stretches beyond infinity's vast expanse,
Contemplating amidst this chaotic world,
settles the heart in a joyful stance.

Out there lies a world so remarkably beautiful,
despite the dirt that may be cast upon it.
In this temporal realm of trials and tribulations,
with His divine mercy,
things are set to unclench our hearts,
like the glimmer of hope
that emanates from babies smiles,
like blooming flowers,

and stars that twinkle bright,
And the people with their hearts shining with light.

Even this place of suffering is crafted with beauty,
to instill hope in those burdened with agony,
to inspire gratitude in those possessors of blessings,
reminding each and everyone
that whatever that surrounds us is beautiful,
for it is created by the Maker of beauty,
a reminder which resonates that,
through the purification of our hearts and souls,
we are destined to become inhabitants,
of a realm of ultimate beauty and serenity,
where suffering ceases and eternal happiness blooms,
a paradise where love knows no end,
and happiness is its air.

13. To the Bazaar of Love

I was a rich merchant,
the owner of the greatest bazaar in my heart.
But then, my bazaar was plundered by the dunya.
They took away everything from me except one:
the Ruh of my existence, the richest of all my riches.
I felt deprived, hungry, and lost,
So I set off on a journey to find provisions
To sustain myself and keep my dreams alive,
I set off to sell my Ruh.

But no place I went to would pay me enough.
Then I met a lonely musafir in the midst of the snow,
And he told me about a bazaar,
for the Ruh I intended to sell.
It was the Bazaar of love,
for which I had traveled across the world in search of.

But I failed to find any bazaar that bought wild souls,
and again I was left hopeless.
Then I crossed paths with the lonely man once again,
And I complained to him that I couldn't find such a market.
But he said to me, 'No, you won't find such a market
in any place you could go to,

But you know The Owner of such a market,
The Owner of love Himself.
Both you and I and this kingdom
belong to Him and Him alone.
In His marketplace, you shall be compensated
everything you ever lost.
For your soul that you would dedicate to Him,
He shall provide you with provisions
that will suffice you until infinity.

Under His will, you shall be a trader once again,
And the bazaar of love
shall be built within your homeland.
There, you shall find shade and companionship
that will bring you peace
and the cold breeze from the flower gardens
of His remembrance into the chambers within you.

And then, in His kingdom, I became a servant.
And in all these lands, I became a stranger.

14. I am but a bedouin

I am but a bedouin,
walking beside the shores of my destiny,
Two destinations for me, one pursued,
the other relentless in pursuit of me.
One shrouded in fear's veil,
the other, a realm of eternal bliss.
One buries me beneath my ephemeral home,
the other, an eternal homeland.

Exhausted, I stumble,
the wind's gentle hand covers me in sand,
A reminder of the closeness of what chases me,
the distance of my yearning.
Shifting dunes conceal the path,
roads fade into oblivion,
The restless sea's crashing waves push me far away.

The pen in my hand, familiar with ink and sweat,
may soon embrace soil, beneath which I shall enjoin.

What I seeks transcends this realm.
And what seeks me is
the gateway to my yearned-for home,
Where all final destinations reside.

All I have to do is keep walking steadfastly on the path,
When the destination chasing me embraces me,
my journey shall complete.
And so I kept walking,
a mere Bedouin, penning this tale,
The pages known only to the One beyond the skies,
the Knower of all destinies.

15. This is not where you and I belong

This is not where you and I belong,
This is where we thrive, not in wealth or fame,
But in the beauty of our soul,
eternal love, and euphoria's flame.

This is the furnace that melts and breaks our hearts,
To etch beautiful patterns, like artworks of divine arts.
Here, we fall in awe with the world's beauty so vast,
Dancing with words of gratitude, in the storms we hold fast.

We look at our scars, our broken pieces with grace,
Through a kaleidoscope's lens, capturing life's embrace.
This place, a prison, a strange land for us strangers,
A rusting place for those who've forgotten their path's dangers.

A testing place for those yearning for faith's sweet scent,
A scent that maps the way to paradise's content.
Do not worry as if the affairs of the dunya are forever,
Remember, everything here is ephemeral;
only hope remains, however.

16. Pursuit of words

I'm in a constant pursuit of words,
words that can eloquently encapsulate
the deep yearnings within my heart,
yearnings that have been boiling
in the pot of sabr within the courtyard of my soul,
yearnings that feels like snowfall
awaiting the gentle touch of dawn
and the warmth of the rising sun
to transform them into a beautiful day.

These yearnings weigh heavily upon me,
that I drag them from the centre of my heart
to the tip of my tongue in duas.
Yearning of how I wish to sit
by the pillars of Medina and to be lost in awe,
yearnings to dwell amidst the
musk-scented mosques of the Arab lands,
yearnings to be chosen to liberate
the smiles of countless hearts
burdened by the weight of dunya.

Yearnings to be at the doorsteps
and then to be a door to a beautiful fragment

of this fleeting dunya that has got the imaginations of
the glimpses of paradise etched upon its skies.
Yearnings to be able to fill a thousand hungry stomachs
and to be the beacon of light
to atleast someone's darkest night.

And I admire them,
those who carry such a yearning in their hearts
that they are only carrying a part within them
while the rest of their heart is drowning
in a deep yearning for Allah's love,
for His paradise and for meeting with beloved ﷺ.

Them those who carry a love
that weighs more than this dunya
within the chambers of their heart.
Them those who are themselves an ocean
from the oceans of goodness.

17. Residents of my heart

The waves reminded me
of myself and some beautiful people
who were once the residents of my heart,
people who used to paint beautiful skies
in the ceilings of the upper chambers.
People who were gardeners in my lawn
and warriors in my battles.
People who were once the caretakers
of the little kid inside of me.
People who had touched my soul
and gave all the beauty to it.

And now the parts of my soul they touched,
are the places where I built museums inside of me.
Now, I am merely a walking gallery of art
that they engraved with laughters and smiles,
a long lost traveler just like these waves that rise
and rush towards the shore to escape drowning,
only to fall back into the ocean of this dunya.

18. This whole world is my museum

I never got to visit museums that are confined within walls
but the whole world is the museum where I go
to behold the chronicles of life and death.
The wrinkle lines, the inscrutable faces,
the sound of the laughters, the waves of the pain,
the depth of the silence, the stories in the eyes,
and even this land that I step on, is a museum piece.

Within the hatred I carry for this world,
within it hidden is a handful of love I have for it,
which just like gravity,
pulls the entire world infront into my eyes,
so that no radiation, no emotion or no light would escape,
to observe it, feel it, learn it, all as a whole,
to explore the mystery behind their entire beingness.
Perhaps it is because I and this entire universe
have the same One creator,
and not an atom exists without a purpose to it.

So now I too, am an admirer of art.
And this whole world is my museum.

19. A Majnun's Qalaam

In seeking closeness to the Rabb of entirety,
we learn that He made even the atoms
as similar to the galaxies of the universe.
He explained with His utmost wisdom,
the superiority of His dominance over the entire creations,
with the most eloquent and beauteous of words
and metaphors in His book,
words that are much deeper than the depth
that any ordinary mind can dive into.

In seek of comprehending the life in this dunya
that He has destined us with,
in contemplating a flawless world
that is being lived by flawed people,
I imagined a world inside of me
where I am merely a wayfarer in the lands of my heart.

The world that my heart is,
has oceans, moons, pretty stars and twinkling clouds,
hefty mountains and deep trenches.
A colossal world whose boundaries are made

not with bricks but with my beliefs.
With gigantic doors and colourful skies.
With pretty gardens as well as stinking slums.
With marvellous castles and roofless huts.
With rivers and waterfalls.

And each time in the places where life puts me,
I imagine myself strolling
through different parts of this heart of mine,
travelling as a stranger to its lands,
creating within me scrolls of lessons
that I learn from within its skies.

A vague attempt to beautify this test
and sufferings that this dunya is,
only to make it to the one ultimate destination of Jannah
with an unshakable spirit. A majnun's qalam,
that attempts to ornament the mundane parts of himself.

20. Mosaic hearts

I marvelled at the mosaic art wall,
and it reminded me
of the walls of the believer's heart,
walls which are adorned
with the colours of all the colourful skies.
Their hearts shatter under the weight of the dunya too,
their fragments do not fall upon dirt
but into vibrant buckets of colors.
With unwavering faith, they gather each piece,
meticulously crafting patterns upon their inner walls,
bonding them with duas,
giving light to them with the remembrance
of the Light of the heaven and the skies.

Every crack within their hearts
look like a crack in the sky
through which a million galaxies
peek into the realms of the eyes,
every sadness in them is like a floating stair,
that takes them to closeness to their Rabb,
every joy within them flows with gratitude,
like rivers that ran away from paradise.

21. The scattered fragments

Amidst all these noises,
why is it that heartbeats, louder than my own,
manage to find their way to my ears?
There are moments when I draw breath,
feeling as though I am inhaling
the scattered fragments of a hundred hearts,
for the very air is infused with the essence of yearnings.

Where the eyes are not to gaze upon are few,
yet what is permissible is infinite,
for there are no boundaries to the expanse of skies,
the warmth of smiles, and the allure of the moon
as seen through countless pairs of eyes.
All of this, He has fashioned with meticulous beauty,
as if seeking to enrapture our spirits and bestow
a rhythm upon the poetry of our souls.

Therefore, turn your gaze not only inward
but also outward to the world,
embracing humility in its fullness,
remembering Him for all moments.

Oh, you bearers of hearts that have wilted,
may both you and I fall upon the fountains of guidance,
get swept away by the currents of faith
onto the path of purpose.
May the weariness that plagues both you and me
find eternal solace in the form of an unyielding spirit,
one that defies the very shackles of life.
Let us confront all challenges with unwavering determination,
fully aware that the One who charted
the course for the moon and stars is the very One
who authored the trajectory of your life and mine.

22. The faces of people

Oyy the faces of people,
if it weren't for your dishonesty,
your masters would have been exposed.

Exposed about the bedlam in their hearts,
and about the thousand worries
that has been robbing of their peace,
and about their beautiful dreams and ruined hopes.

You guard their hearts,
but the two pretty eyes in you are transparent enough.
Those eyes weren't awestruck
by the beauty of the skies
but lost in the heaviness of their affairs.
Those eyes can't mask the despair that
the facade made of pretentious emotions hide.

People who sit in the corners of these streets
and are lost in the vastness of their own worlds,
and yearns to speak out but
the words die at the tip of the lips,
may you find solace in The One who knows
the language of your heart and the weight of your breaths.

May you attain the lightness in the chest
by entrusting your affairs in the hands of The One
who is the ultimate manager of affairs.
May your pain taste like sweet sherbet in your heart
and may your happiness turn into a river of gratitude
in the meadows within your soul.

23. Tapestry of life

In tapestry of life, we reside,
Where blessings bestowed will someday hide.
From our hand's gentle grasp
to above the white clouds,
or beneath the dark soil, where secrets lie.

A time shall come, when the world's weight,
shall be lifted off, and our souls elate.
Our essence shall be entwined
with the soil's embrace,
reuniting once again as willed by the divine.

The giver, The All-wise,
takes what's given, to give some better prize.
Transforming sufferings, in a magnificent array,
offering something better, lighting our way.

There is no separation,
from those laid to rest in the black Earth,
but a temporary parting,
until we meet again, in the destiny to be weaved,
together forever, hearts never to leave.

24. Guilt

I am guilty of many a thing that I admit of doing.
I stole from the emotions that the waves bought to the shores
along with the sand that got stuck under my feet.
I eavesdropped the whispers of the wind
by placing my hand over my ears.

I fled away from many hearts and places
where I found myself alone in midst of a crowd.
I saw tears falling down their cheeks
but it fell upon my lands that I felt half of their pain.
I saw smiles in their faces that
were powerful enough to brew tears in my eyes.

I carry within me a library of fragrances
that I took away from books and people,
and from the wind, clouds and the stars.
I stole poetry from their eyes and from the moon's light.
I admire windows but I built walls
upon the broken parts of myself.
I burn not wood but words inside my heart
to keep it warm from the cold outside.

I smell sea waves and coffee each time

I hold a pen to draw pictures with words.
I looked for the keys to the doors that were left unlocked.
I want to sow my name not in gardens nor
ln nameplates but in their prayers.

25. People of the streets

Oh, dear people of the streets,
how I long to offer you more than
this feeble smile of mine.
When I gaze into your eyes,
I witness the same desolate emptiness
one finds in the eyes of those
who have lost their homeland.

And your eyes hurts my heart.
I don't know the depth of your grief
nor the genuineness of your pain,
but your hands that is being extended to me
which I reject in helplessness disgraces my soul.

Within your cold countenance,
I see a heart that has hardened after enduring
countless trials and tribulations.
In the depths of your famished stomach,
I see the burial ground of your forgotten, unwatered soul.

However, here I am,
walking away from you,
feeling more unfortunate than you,

for I am still unable to express
gratitude for all that I possess,
constantly in complain.
Yet, you, in accepting your fate,
find solace in silence.

26. The ones who can craft stars

And then there are the ones who can craft stars
and hang them at the top of your heart.
The ones who can keep the clouds afloat
and bring waves of warmth into you,
as cozy as a coffee on a winter evening.

The ones whose words are so marvelous
that you wish to know what
the inside of their head and heart would look like.
The ones who will bring the lamp to you
amidst the darkest of nights,
the ones with whom you are blessed
to share the same part of the dunya and wish
to share the same part in the valleys of Paradise.

The inhabitants of your heart and of your prayers.

May Allah increase the number of such individuals for you,
to the point where you can no longer name each of them.
May there be so many
that they become a nation in your heart.

27. A mirror to this sky

Some days I look at these skies
within the light in my eyes
and whisper to myself that,
only if the whole of my heart
could be a mirror to this entire sky,
only then I would be able to hold
within myself all the stars that I wish
to own inside of me.

I feel a yearning right in the midst of my heart,
a yearning to be a part of these clouds,
of these clouds that ornaments the skies of the world,
and the poems of the poets
and the hearts of the dreamers.
Have you noticed them,
the clouds who are constantly in motion
despite darkness periodically taking over them,
so sure that the golden rays
of the sun shall once again touch them
and they shall once again turn beautiful.

I wish my heart to be the same too,
to be constantly in motion towards my Rabb,

seeking refugee in Him all along the darkness,
with complete assurance about His plans
and a tawakkul in Him about
how the light from Him shall come
and illuminate the darkest parts of my life once again.

These clouds that turn dark out of despair,
heavier out of their burden,
have you seen them pouring out
their pain away as rain,
into the lands and to the oceans.
I wish for my heart to be same,
to pour out its heaviness
into the ground in prostration.

I wish for my heart to be as this cloud in the sky,
to be a beautifully woven part
floating in a serene bright soul
that extends all over the horizons of my mindfulness.

28. A dream train

And I dream of boarding a train
from the farthest corner of that place,
right besides the largest of the gates.
A train that passes through the vast gardens
of perpetual residence and hefty palaces.
A train which halts at the homes
of them the noblest of men.
A train which passes over the scented rivers of paradise
and by the side of the springs of blessings.
A train whose length is infinite and whose passengers
are the Righteous and the Repentant.

And I dream to enter in it
with all the people I know and loved.
I dream of this train that ends at the doorsteps
of the residence of the Most Beloved to Allah,
at the home of Muhammad ﷺ.
And to meet with him,
the one who carried the love
for his people beyond time.
To greet him with peace,
this time shaking his hands
and looking at his face.

To hear his voice. And to hug him.
Perhaps this being among the greatest
of bounties of the paradise.

And I walk in here to cover the large distance
between me and these dreams of mine.
And may my weak heart be warned of the thorns
that might bleed me on the way,
so that my drops of blood and sweat can be a witness
to how I passed through this journey.

29. People who feel like a prayer

Prayer mats are amongst
the most beautiful places on Earth.
They adorn the pieces of lands on Earth
upon which the weights
of the heavy hearts are unloaded.
They hear the whispers of
the ailing heart and of the weeping servant.

But there are even more beauteous prayer mats
that are deeply hidden in the hearts
of people who are suffering in this dunya.
People who are constantly in
conversation with their beloved Lord,
sharing with Him about
every trials and every worries,
with their eyes brimming out of
gratitude for every blessings.

People who pray for even every
unknown soul that they come across,
people who would magically turn

every blessing and every pain into prayers,
so that anything that afflicts them
gets transformed into a bounty for them,
people who are themselves a prayer mat
that reflects so much of serenity
and carries a love for the whole world.

People who cleans their hearts with their tears
and polishes it with the remembrance
of the One who ought to be remembered always.

I wonder how walking into their heart would feel like,
whether it'll be like getting into a garden
filled with all those pretty scented flowers,
or would it feel like gazing at a moonlit sky full of stars.

I wish I lived in a country full of such people.
I wish I get to be among a crowd of such people.
I wish I get to be a companion of one of those people.
I wish I could turn out to be one among those people.
Those people who feel like a yearning to remember God.
Those people who feel like a prayer.

30. I returned back to the prayer mat

I returned back to the prayer mat,
the land where I celebrate the reunion
of all the fragments of myself that fallen of me
while traversing through dunya.

I returned to the prayer mat and
every sad thing inside of me turned beautiful.
Every pain turned into joy.
Every breath felt like breathing in an entire constellation.

Flowers started to grow on my flawed walls
and the pain that came with the heartache suddenly
bursted into fireworks in my sky of hopefulness.
Tears rushed to put out the flame
that was burning me from the inside out.

I put my head down, but it was my heart that fell down
and got sunk into the deep earth.
I touched my forehead on the ground,
but I felt touching the windowpanes
of my heart from withn the inside.

The heaviness that sunk me in the dark oceans of the dunya
suddenly vanished and I found myself floating
above every places where I once drowned.
I found myself flowing as a river that seeks
to join the ocean of the ones who seeks paradise.

31. Senses

They said hearts were caged within bodies,
but I don't feel mine in there anymore,
all I hear is the music of the waves,
for it cruising in the oceans,
seeking for places that has never been found.

They said it was the heart that was beating,
while it was the soul that was
actually knocking at the doors,
to let it out from this rusted body.

The eyes that looked at words got lost in worlds.
The limbs kept on walking
but the soul never moved from certain places
that felt like a thousand years.
The arms that cannot lift the weights of this waves
were already carrying worlds in their palms .

It was in the most silent moments that
my ears bled off the loudness of the noise.

The world is weird and a pretty lie my dear,
it lies beyond what the eyes see,

beyond what the senses sense,
it lies beyond our perceptions and imaginations,
it lies within a power that created even the time.

A mind that runs on that timeline won't be sufficient
to process the powers of the One who is omnipotent.
So all we do today, is to be patient and to have trust.

32. What we yearn for

At times, this tingling in the heart,
and this cold breeze in the lungs,
is what we yearn for in this Dunya.

The feel of the lungs filled to the fullest
and the body carrying the soul
with a sense of serene pride,
a pride not on achievements
but a pride on trusting, how in the end
everything shall go well.

A sense of hope,
a courage of fearlessness of the outcomes,
a confidante who is the Almighty,
a goal which is endless, a pursuit of excellence,
a scent of happiness, all warming the heart.

To walk around with wide smiles
and feel like spawning fowers in gardens
and carrying rainbows above our heads.
To be strong enough to stop the wind
and weak enough to be imprisoned by a child's smile.

33. Dirt

I was worried about the dirt
that was on my white thobe,
but have I ever been worried
about the dirt that is inside of me,
in every corner of my heart?

I cleaned my home, but have I even thought
about cleaning my heart that has now turned
into a landfill of garbage,
with stinking words and rotting thoughts?
Have the dirt that has fallen on the floor
ever reminded me, of the dirt that is
going to be thrown over my body when
I shall be put down in my burial home, left to be alone?

Have I ever thought about the dirt that is going to stain
the white cloth in which I shall be wrapped,
while I was brushing off the dirt
from that white shirt of mine?

Have I ever been worried
about the dirt that is going to eat
every part of me, the same very parts

that accompanied me to every corner of this dunya,
the parts that were held hostage
by a mind that was away from its Rabb?

A temporal journey, from dirt to dirt,
from a womb to a graveyard,
yet how forgetful have I been,
drifting away from truth,
falling prey to the illusions of a dunya
that will only tear my heart
like how the thorns of a rose tears
the palm Of the one who held it with love.

34. An ocean of blessings

They look upon these lands as a hopeless,
barren desert, oblivious to the fact that it is here
that Allah's mercy cascades like never-ending rain,
transforming every inch into an ocean of blessings.
Once separated from this vast expanse,
they find themselves gasping for air,
yearning for the richness they left behind.

Glad tidings to those who appreciate this divine rain,
who reach out and collect a handful of its drops.
Glad tidings to those who humbly bow their heads in sujood,
creating ripples and waves in this ocean of blessings,
making their gratitude felt and heard throughout the skies.

It is impossible to imagine without awe how
Allah must be smiling upon His beloved servant,
whose heart throbs and eyes shed tears
in anticipation of the goodness that has
already been written in their destinies.

How magnificent will be the joy
of a heart that embraces the goodness
it has longed for and always yearned.

Truly, this is a land of blessings,
experienced by the ungrateful.
And the other side of here is a land of misery,
experienced by the innocent.

35. Righteous companion

A righteous companion is like a twinkling star
in the dark blue skies, holding the hands
of a lost sailor. A bond not bound by blood
nor bounties but by a love for the sake of Allah.

A warmth in the heart and coolness in the eyes,
just as we seek in our duas. One with whom
you can share the pangs of your heart,
trying to bridge the choices of dunya and
yearnings for the Aakhirah.

A yusr in the 'usr of dunya, a shoulder to support
when you stumble, a pair of palms raised
in the last third of nights, mentioning your name
to the Malik of this entire Mulk.

A pair of eyes that see through your heart
when you feel inexistent in the corners where
the dunya pushes you, a blessing like flowers
honoring the gardens of the heart.

A bond, at least half as beautiful
as that between the Sahabahs and Nabi ﷺ

36. Remove your armours

Remove your armours,
for it slows you down.
Move out of your stone castles,
for it wears you off.
Neither iron walls nor shields shall protect you
from the scars of the fate that awaits you.

O the bearer of a heart that is
a wayfarer to the rest of the dunya,
hop on your horses and gallop
through the shores of destiny,
cutting through the waves of gloom
and the winds of glee,
aiming to conquer all the peaks in your dream lands.

For not in fear but in unshakable pursuit
shall we find out the path,
to that place which eludes the confines of maps,
to that place where all the senses
inside of us shall find a home.

That path which is not made of roads or stoned,
but rather forged by hearts that serves

as a moon to all the planets of faith,
which carry within them a sanctuary
where solacew shall be found.

Our destination is not upon the land
nor amidst the clouds,
but in a realm where only a pure heart
can perceive its ethereal presence.
The colours of our land can be felt
in the kaleidoscopic hues that adorn the skies.

A place so mysterious ,
that the path leading there lies
scattered amidst the bustling streets,
within the depths of the chosen hearts,
and upon the sacred prayer mats
where devout souls seek solace.

37. I looked at the moon

I looked at the moon
from the top of these mountains
and thought of my heart
that is as much as distant
deep inside my existence
surrounded by a vacuum of numbness.
This piece of flesh which is imprisoned within me,
it once tasted the sweetness of closeness to its Rabb
and now, whenever I hitchhike
through the chaos of this dunya,
it aches, it pains as if it is
being pulled out and torn away.

A step away from that sweetness
aches so much that it burns
and cause a wildfire inside my soul.
I turn into dust in these warlands,
and gets carried away by the waves
whenever I float away from faith.

My own emptiness burdens me
and my silence wounds me.

And what shall I do when I am a stranger
in all these places and to all these people,
except to talk to the One who knows my destiny?
And how loud these people
shout but they are left unheard,
while my whispers go beyond all the skies.

A mind that wrote stories in all the places it went to
has now become a mind that
never can stop thinking about
how Allah might have written the stories
of all these places and people.

A heart that was attached to people
has now been torn away from them
and thrown above the skies to seek for its Rabb.
A soul that was restless has now become
a resident on the banks of a river of mercy
that originates from the Most Merciful.

I have now become a strange traveler,
and now I travel to faraway lands
only to enjoin them the strangers who are blessed
with the glad tidings of the paradise.

38. Yearning for Medinah

There's a place that I yearn to visit,
a place which holds a part of heaven,
a place I'm not even worthy to approach.

No words that I weave, nor the gleam in my eyes,
will be enough to describe the beauty
of the fragrance of this wonderland.

The morning breeze fondled my soul,
lifting it high as if to the skies,
and the first glimpse of this place
reduced the innocent me to tears.

It felt like a snowfall in my heart
as I sat gazing at its dome.
I fell down and was stumped upon by people
when I was about to step into that piece of heaven.

I tried to memorize every pattern and pillar,
aim to etch the beauty of that castle forever.
My heart ached, and I cried when I had to leave
that magnificent land.

I witnessed it years ago,
but now, at times, I feel the weight of those moments.
I melt each time the memories
of seeing that place hit me.

I hear its name, and I'm transported back in time
to those days when I was physically there.
I can once again feel every breath of mine in that place,
filled with regrets for not being able to love
my beloved Prophet ﷺ and the beauty of his home enough.

Despite all the filth that has darkened me from within,
a small fragment of my heart fell off
in that land the last time I visited.
Each time I hear the name of that place,
each time I hear 'Medinah,' it feels like
I'm hearing about a long-lost home.

I yearn from the depths of my being to return,
to the land where I felt the most peaceful,
to the land that heals every wounded soul
and rejuvenates every broken heart.

I wish I were blessed to be an inhabitant of Medinah,
so I could have lived the happiest of lives.

39. I am a plant

The soil upon which I am a sprouted plant,
this soil is not nourished merely by the rain
but by the unsung tears and sweats
of the ones who bought me up.

The perfume that I carry along with me,
is brewed from the sweat of a man
who built up an empire in his heart for us to live in luxury.
No moonlit night could sink my heart
in a puddle of love more than the sight of the light
in my mother's eyes when she wears a joyful smile.

I came from them in fragments,
and I took from them fragments.
My fathers arms wrapped
around me before I took a fall
and my mothers hand soothed my aches,
by the will of the Rabb.

And now, with time, with wrinkles and with grey hairs,
they have turned into a beautiful heart ache within me.
For the fortress in which they hosted me as a prince,
I pray for them to be the owners

of a fortress in the highlands of Jannah.
And I pray to be a tree which could provide a shade for them,
just like how they provided a shade for me
whilst it was burning and snowing outside.
I cannot settle my heart anywhere
but in the places where they'd happy.

40. Beautiful destinies

How beautiful are the destinies of the ones
who are destined to be the soil of the lands
upon which people shall find their way back to Allah.
The ones that Allah chose to guide people's hearts
towards the infinite ocean of His love and mercy.

The ones who are blessed with eloquence in their presence,
the ones through whom the sweet scent of this faith
shall spread to the lost souls.
The littlest of acts which sometimes sprouts
in the deserted hearts, the seeds of guidance,
and the ones who are chosen to deliver them,
how blessed their affairs are.

Every guidance is from Allah alone,
and to be a vessel which pours
to put out the fire in the hearts
and fills it with divine love,
would be such a great purpose to live for.

To be a faint little star in a dark sky
that guides the lost sailor.

To be a kite that flies away in the direction
of the path which ends up in Jannah.

41. Parts of Dunya

Sometimes, some parts of dunya grows into us.
Our homes, our cars, the places where we found peace,
that favourite accessories that we use, the dreams,
certain people we get so much used to in our lives,
all the places where we walked and lived happily as a kid,
those kids that carries a love for us in their eyes.

Apart from all our flaws and restlessness in here,
there are certain things in here
we wish to carry with ourselves.
Not that we are assured of Jannah,
but I imagine people might carry
all these parts to Jannah too,
as a memoir of their past life,
to carry every joyous parts of here
to the world of eternal joy.

42. Distances

How Allah displays
the notion of distances is too beautiful.
He placed the burning stars,
the whirling moons, and the planets,
and all those objects made of stardust
in absolute distance from the eyes,
made everything appear
too beautiful from the distance.

The dreams and the goals of all
the longing hearts are beautiful too,
when they are too far away
to be held in the palms,
but their beauty faints within the arms.

And the distance between us and our beloved ones
and all the places we love,
brings a pressing pain that is felt
right in the depth of the heart.
And sometimes this same distance
when reduced to six feet below the ground,
comes with a pain that is unbearable.

But then Allah with His mercy
blessed us with forgetfulness,
where we forget about all the distances
that exist between us,
and all the things of the universe.

He made a dimension where
distances go beyond perceptions.
Allah made the distance between us
and everything that we yearn for,
as short as an answered prayer.

Even if the distance between us
and the remembrance of Him is too far,
He made it in such a way that a single step
back would take us back to Him.

And Allah placed everything in different corners
separated by vast distances, and sufferings and obstacles
so that when we walk upon here,
seeking a quench to the thirst and
a matter to fill the voids of our heart,
the distance between us and Him slowly disappears.

43. Letters to himself

He used to write letters to himself and leave them by the doorside of his home before he left to roam around the world. And one day when he was asked why, he said,

"No matter what I built within me,
I know that dunya will surely break it
into pieces and crumbles it.
I know that dunya will shatter
the coloured glasses inside of me
and wound me with it. So I turn my voice
into words in these letters,
where I remind myself about
how I built mansions within me,
about how I melted mountains and forged iron
and how I healed the wounds without leaving scars,
so that I won't forget that,
all of the inside of me could be fixed
once again when I return back."

And one of his letters was found which read,
"Oyy Abd'Allah!
How many times have you quit in your life?
How many times have you felt exhausted

and have given up on that which once took away
your sleep and stole your breaths?
How many times have you forgotten
the blessings that you have been poured with?
How many times have you forgotten 'who you are',
'what you are capable of', 'why you are here'?
Is this small atom of weight the thing that
sinks your great heart that is being entrusted to you?

Have you forgotten your duty,
the faces of your beloved ones, the span of your wishes?
Will these moving time make you motionless?
Will this tiredness find a home inside of you
while there is a fire to be lit in you?
Will this grief be permanent guest in you while
you can't afford enough to feed the happiness in you?

Wake up beloved one, the sun has risen and so did you,
and you got a lot to do. You got to run every road
to find the pathway to your destination.
You got to be tireless in your pursuits,
fearless in your darkness, boundless in your dreams.
You got to clean your heart with the entire ocean
and fill your lungs with the entire skies.
You got to stand up and fight the world.
You got to be unstoppable when you walk
towards the doors which have been open to you.

Don't lie down, stand up and go,
go towards your destiny, towards your dreams,
towards seeking whatever that is worthy to be sought,
towards all the colourful places of the world
where you could see the glimpses of hope,
the beauty of faith and the greatness of your Rabb"

44. O the blessed month

Each day pass by as if I take
one more step to walk into my homeland.
I feel as a weary pilgrim who has finally
arrived at the door steps of a holy land.

O the blessed month, O Ramadan,
you are the land that I have been
searching for without even a map,
you are the land into which
I wish to get imprisoned in,
you are the land of which
I wish to be a part of.

You arrive and everything here change
into its most beautiful self.
You are like the first rain after a dreadful drought.
You arrive just like how the sun rise,
spreading your rays and giving hope to a land
that was left under the darkness.
You arrive and the hearts fill up with serenity.
You arrive and the thirst of the rotting soul is quenched,
and the ailing hearts are healed,
and the people take the pain with honour,

expecting ease soon from their Rabb.

You arrive and the poor is helped in abundance,
you arrive and the masjids are full,
and the recitation of Qur'an resonates
in and around the houses and the buildings,
and the beautiful stories of Prophets are discussed,
and the relatives are visited,
and the hearts break free from the chains
of the manipulating world, to connect to its Rabb.

The heart now bangs on the walls with happiness,
with tears and with a book full of prayers
that it wishes to whisper
in the days and nights of this blessed month.

45. The street of Ramadan

I have been walking around the street of Ramadan,
the most delightful of streets, where the sky is adorned
with a wide opened Baab Ar-Rayyan,
and all the gates of the hell are closed.
The air here is scented with a yearning for paradise
and a fear of the grave and the fire of Hell.

And through the middle of the street,
flows a river of the God's mercy,
by the banks of which the inhabitants
wash the dirt upon their hearts.
And in the corners,
kept are big mirrors which reflects
not the outer appearance but the inner self.

The words of the God are its melody,
tears are its streams, time is its currency,
righteous deeds its goods. Ikhlas is its language,
Dua is its sherbet, dhikr is its sweet.
Taqwa is its government, and those who put holes
to the bags of Eemaan are its prisoners.
And it has a school of Sabr for its inhabitants,
and a hospital of Eemaan for

the ones who are broken-hearted.

It is such a street that a heart that finds a home
in here shall never settle in any other place.
It is such a street that the eyes
that truely witnessed every part of it
shall never see any beauty in rest of the world.
It is the street where the fruits and flowers
of generosity blooms in the gardens
of those who are in need.
It is a street where the rain of Tawakkul
shall extinguish the fire of the burning heart.

It is such a street that each step taken in it
lifts the inhabitants a step closer to the God.
It is such a street that even the dead and
the hardened heart is melted and renovated.
It is such a street that every visitor is clothed
with the garments of God-consciousness
and every soul is fed with
the most luscious dish of divine love.
It is the only street where the beggars are the most successful,
where the slaves feel content,
where the ornaments of the world goes meaningless.

It is a street from which parting away
is saddening for the visitors.

It is a street which gives homes
to many who feel homeless.
It is a street which feels like a shady tree
right in the midst of a scorching sun.
It is a street which many hearts
patiently waits and yearn for.
It is a street that bids farewell.

It is a street which has the road
to Jannah in its farthest end.

46. To the waves of tribulations

O beloved one, I, too, am a witness
to the waves of tribulations that have rushed
and struck the shores of our homeland,
erasing the smiles and happiness
we once drew upon the sand.

I never forget how we always sought refuge
in Allah's mercy when the waves took pieces
from within us and from those who journeyed alongside.
We learned how the waves would always recede,
and how our weakened parts shall regain strength,
and how the heart that shrank will always once again bloom,
all when we place our trust in Him alone.

And now, when you say that you have given up
on the fortress of duas you have made,
it shakes the whole in me.
The endless suffering that cracks
every corner of your heart
hurts me more than your own pain.

As I witness you wither under the weight of hardships,
I restrain my filled eyes and my trembling voice,
longing to reignite within you the light
that always reminded us of the divine,
of how He turned this place into a realm of endurance,
and how He tests those He loves.

How can you be the beloved of the Lord of the Universe
and give up on His love? How can you drown in these waves
when within you lies a lightness that keeps you afloat
amidst the miseries of this worldly life?
A lightness destined to carry you to the realms of Jannah.
How can this fleeting world weigh you down
when you hold the gardens of the eternal world
upon your tongue, within your heart,
and within your dreams?

All these hardships shall come to an end
in the best possible way, and once again,
you shall find solace, for your destiny is penned
by the most perfect of writers. In His words,
you shall discover a home and hope.

Whispers to God

And as I reached the midway of his diary, there was a beautifully decorated title page which read "Whispers to God." And then suddenly a musk-scented wind blew across the caravans that were crossing the majestic deserts of this dunya, reminding one of how, in between these barren lands, there lies comfort in the remembrance of the Divine.

Each word, a prayer, a sigh, a plea, A dialogue with the One, unseen yet so near. Through trials and triumphs, joy and despair, The inked expressions, a heartfelt affair.

The pen danced across the parchment, Scripting tales of a seeker, in moments fervent.

The diary unfolded, a sacred odyssey, A seeker's journey, in pursuit of eternity. So I kept reading, from amongst his pieces of letters to the Rabb.

47. Golden clouds

O Allah, The One who burns the hearts of the believers to bring light to its chambers, I beg you to never deprive me of the light that calms my soul and guides me to the straight path, that path which is taken by those who are loved by You.

O Allah, The writer of my destiny, The Owner of time, You have all the wisdom of my past and my future, I beg You to have my destiny always end while I am traversing towards You and never away from You.

O the Light of the Heavens and the Earth, You have made this faith as beautiful as the blue skies, and You created certain people's heart as pure as the white fluffy clouds. And when the rays of Your guidance collides with their precious hearts, they turn into something that is as exquisite as the golden clouds that adorn the sunrise and sunset skies. Make my heart among such hearts. Make my soul among such souls.

O Allah, I am among them those travellers who walk around the vast lands inside their hearts and build castles and museums for moments and memories, I am among them those who go war in the war-lands within oneself, I am among those who yearn to seek to praise Your ultimate wisdom in every existence in both the ground and the skies, and I beg You my Rabb, do not let me sink into the lands within myself and get lost into darkness, do not let me be hopeless despite being only a wayfarer on the lands of Your mercy, do not let me be among those who have been destined to be deprived of the scent of the magnificent gardens that You have prepared for the righteous and the repentant. Align the rhythm of my heart to the resonance of a love that is for You Alone.

48. An unshakable castle

Each time I talk to You my Rabb, I feel the speaker inside myself sitting down on a plain barren land whose borders cover all the horizons.

O Allah, shower the seeds of guidance, of contentment and of blessings onto these lands where I found the way to You so that they turn into beautiful gardens, gardens where I could find a home right in the midst of here where only You, are the watcher and the listener.

Ya Rabb, each drop of tears that I shed and each time I moist my tongue for the sake of You, replace them for me with beautiful rivers of your mercy flowing through the courtyard of my heart so that it thrives flowers of taqwa in me.

You have guided me with the destination, and now I request You my Rabb, guide me towards the people who share the same destination with me, the destination of Jannah.

You know my weaknesses, turn me into an unshakable castle whose walls are decorated with the smiles of being content with what You have destined for me.

I come to you with my absolute weaknesses and inabilities and my burden of sins, I yield each of the pangs of my heart to call out Your names, Ya Rahman guide me in every single step of mine, protect me in my each breath and strengthen me from both the in and the out and with Your mercy help me be worthy of carrying a love for You in the chambers of my heart and let its fragrance be my beauty and let its light be that guides my eyes.

49. A million stars have spawned

Oh Allah, I have been blinded by the colors of the dunya. I have disgraced my soul with ignorance and ungratefulness. I have been on a path that turns away from the path of those whom You love.

But, by Your mercy, You have opened my eyes, from darkness to light, as if a million stars have spawned into my darkest skies. The moon, which I carried as a symbol of love, fell on my desert and melted into an ocean of my love towards You, my Rabb. I have fortified my walls against the dunya, and I have started to reclaim the parts of myself that have been left out and taken by people, all to raise the flag of submission to You, my Rabb.

You know the depth of every wound in me long before I even felt it, and when I walk inwardly ailing, the only distance between all my pain and its solace is the distance between my heart and Your remembrance. I walk this road to join the path of those who walk towards You. On my journey, I pray that all the hearts that collide with my eyes become a means of bringing me closer to Your path, my Rabb. I pray that all the burdens that tire me make me strong enough to push through the walls that lie in the midst of my way towards You.

I pray that You always preserve this beautiful sky for my eyes so that I will never forget the beauty of the destination I am walking to.

50. That day

I was downhearted,
but then You woke me up to yet another beautiful day,
and filled up my lungs with the fragrance of Your love,
and brought ecstasy to the shores of my heart.

My heart, just like a horse,
was galloping through the desert of my sorrow,
but then You placed an oasis of compassion
in midst of my barren land, to quench my thirst for serenity.

And inside of it You displayed the moon to me,
the very moon that brings
sparkles to the eyes and glee to the hearts,
the very moon whose reflections were so blessed
to fall upon the eyes of our beloved Prophet ﷺ,
and that moon brought smiles to my pale face.

Then You gave warmth to my soul with
the coldness of mornings after my tiring nights.
And then You showed to me how

You magnificently unfurls the day from within the darkness
by bringing the golden rays of the sun to the dark blue skies,
giving hope to my heart to rise.

You placed fog upon my path, only to slowly
and magically unveil the beauty of Your plans.
Both my hands and my legs froze
by the coldness of this wind that You blew upon me,
but by Your mercy I lit up a fireplace in my heart
to radiate warmth to my soul and to shed light
to my chambers so that I won't go astray
from the path towards You in the darkness.

51. A door which opens to infinity

And when my soul feel like being
withered away from my being,
and when my heart hardens
under the flame of this world,
and when my limbs and all my senses feel weakened,
that is when You push me down on my knees
and reminds my soul, asking "Have you forgotten me?".

When I wandered around this dunya
in search of a door to exit,
I found that I was already by the doorsteps
of a door which opens to infinity,
a path that takes the traveler to You my Rabb,
to You whose knowledge encompasses
everything that ever existed and ever will.

And in there You willed to teach me how
You take away the seeds of the fruits that You give me,
only to sow it in the most perfect of time,
so that it'll be the tree that gives me

the shade when I grow tired.

Your wisdom is absolute while mine is inexistent.
Your plans are unsurpassed while mine are worthless.
I cried to You of how I am pointlessly floating
around this world where You sent me,
and getting hurt by the corners of this world,
but then You wrapped me in more grief
so that I'll find the warmth of Your love
at the bottom of my heart when I fall down helplessly.

You drown me in my own misery
so that I'll witness the sparkles of the pearls of wisdom
that you hide behind every worry of mine.
Your love cannot be measured
for Yours is the epitome of Love,
the absolute love, for You are the creator of love.
And where would I go to, if not to You,
to mend my broken heart and feed my tired soul?

52. You are the One who knows

Ya Rabb, I walk upon all these lands but You are the one who knows which of these would be the graveyard where I along with my memories shall be buried.

If my heart was seen as a mountain, You are the one who knows beyond even the atoms of the grains out of which it was made. If my soul was seen as an ocean, You are the one who knows about it more than the number of droplets that united to form it.

You gave free will to my nafs, but I wish all my wills were only for the sake of Your love. I speak and write so, but I fail in my attempts and falls into darkness, but then You are the one who picks me up and gives me light and hope.

Ya Rabb, give me strength to push away these walls that comes closer and closer and suffocates me. Give me strength to keep hold of my fleeting mind so that I can flee away from anything that tries to imprison me.

Pain

"And tonight I met the poet in my heart,
sitting upon a solitary dune
that the wind never fondled in the midst of the desert.
I asked him why was he alone and he replied,
"I was the gatekeeper of a graveyard of memories,
of both happiness and sadness,
but then I saw Gaza,
and all the places that belonged to me,
turned into a graveyard in which I buried
the images of the innocent faces of the children of Gaza
along with my sorrows and grief,
a vast land that is expanding in bound
and occupying all the place that surrounds me.""

The book has been compiled during the heart wrenching pain of the people of Palestine. And when you reach this page, let it remind you for your sincere prayers for them and all those who are oppressed around the world. May Allah protect them and ease their affairs.

Gratitude And Duas

Dear Reader,

Thank you, for embarking on this spiritual journey with "Whispers to God." Your presence on this path means the world to me. May the words within these pages resonate with your hearts and bring moments of reflection and peace into your lives.

As we part ways , I express my deepest gratitude to Allah, the Source of all inspiration and wisdom. May His blessings be upon you, enveloping you in tranquility, guiding you on your journey, and showering your life with divine light. In your reflections, may you find clarity, In your struggles, may you find strength, In your joys, may you find gratitude.

You could always express your sincere reviews, doubts and corrections for the book through my instagram: @lifeofmajnun or through an email at rasinbinabdulla@gmail.com.

With sincere appreciation,
Razin

www.ingramcontent.com/pod-product-compliance
Lightning Source LLC
LaVergne TN
LVHW041113150826
845673LV00007B/2041

9798896998617